This Quiet

JOURNAL

belongs to:

_____

Some of our greatest ideas, art, and inventions—from the theory of evolution to van Gogh's sunflowers to the personal computer—came from quiet and cerebral people who knew how to tune in to their inner worlds and the treasures to be found there.

INTRODUCTION

"The quieter you become, the more you can hear."

BABA RAM DASS, SPIRITUAL TEACHER

I am fascinated by introversion—and the power that inheres in it—but I wasn't expecting my book *Quiet* to reverberate quite so forcefully. I'm grateful that it has. And I'm indebted to the many readers who have come forward with their own stories of sometimes feeling out of place in a world that seems to worship what I call the Extrovert Ideal. What's evident in their stories is how much the world has to gain by recognizing the gifts that come with an inward focus.

Many of us have spent years ignoring our preferences and overlooking our strengths. We have been interrupted, spoken over, persuaded into going along with other people's plans and ideas. But we have also possessed great powers, tended deep friendships, and lived beautiful lives.

With this journal, I wish you the chance to explore and develop the strengths of your own temperament. The prompts will help you reconsider some of your existing ideas about shyness and introversion, lead you to uncover your hidden assets, and guide you to make incremental changes that will dramatically increase your energy.

I invite you to answer these questions and work through the exercises without worrying too much about what you write. Don't overthink your answers. It doesn't matter how things sound. This journal is a private space, and in our highly digitized lives, that's a rare thing. Embrace it. No one will read your responses. No one will offer a thumbs-up or counter opinion. It's not worth coming up with a polished answer to any given prompt, because in that polish, you'd lose something of your inner voice, and *that's* the voice you need to listen to.

By giving yourself the quiet time necessary for any journaling practice, you're already ahead of the game. This inner journey is one you have to take alone, but there are many of us walking quietly on our own paths—right beside you.

SUSAN CAIN

"In a gentle way, you can shake the world."

MAHATMA GANDHI,
INDIAN SOCIAL ACTIVIST AND WRITER

A MANIFESTO FOR INTROVERTS

1

There's a word for "people who are in their heads too much:" *thinkers.*

2

Solitude is a catalyst for innovation.

3

The next generation of quiet kids can and must be raised to know their own strengths.

4

Sometimes it helps to be a pretend extrovert. There will always be time to be quiet later.

5

In the long run, staying true to your temperament is the key to finding work you love and work that matters.

6

One genuine new relationship is worth a fistful of business cards.

7

It's okay to cross the street to avoid making small talk.

8

"Quiet leadership" is not an oxymoron.

9

Love is essential: gregariousness is optional.

I.

FINDING YOUR QUIET

—

ASSESSING WHERE YOU ARE

OUR LIVES ARE SHAPED as profoundly by personality as by gender or race. And one of the most important aspects of personality is where we fall on the introvert-extrovert spectrum. Our place on this continuum influences our choice of friends and mates and how we make conversation, resolve differences, and show love. It affects the careers we choose and whether or not we succeed at them. It influences how likely we are to exercise, commit adultery, function well without sleep, learn from our mistakes, place big bets in the stock market, delay gratification, be a good leader, and ask "what if."

Your Personality

The better you understand your nature, the better chance you have of finding the unique gifts you have to offer the world. The following pages will guide you toward understanding your personality. We all have to do things that don't come naturally . . . some of the time. But it shouldn't be all the time. It shouldn't even be most of the time.

What kinds of thoughts and activities come naturally to you?

_____

_____

_____

_____

_____

_____

_____

_____

_____

_____

_____

_____

_____

_____

_____

_____

_____

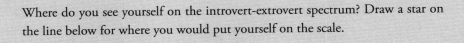

Where do you see yourself on the introvert-extrovert spectrum? Draw a star on the line below for where you would put yourself on the scale.

EXTREME INTROVERT ⟵——————————⟶ EXTREME EXTROVERT

Mark where you think others perceive you on this spectrum.

EXTREME INTROVERT ⟵——————————⟶ EXTREME EXTROVERT

THE FOLLOWING QUESTIONS CAN HELP YOU get a better sense of how introverted or extroverted you might be. Answer each question "true" or "false," choosing the answer that applies to you more often than not.

INTROVERT-EXTROVERT QUIZ

1. _____ I prefer one-on-one conversations to group activities.
2. _____ I often prefer to express myself in writing.
3. _____ I enjoy solitude.
4. _____ I seem to care less than my peers about wealth, fame, and status.
5. _____ I dislike small talk, but I enjoy talking in depth about topics that matter to me.
6. _____ People tell me that I'm a good listener.
7. _____ I'm not a big risk-taker.
8. _____ I enjoy work that allows me to "dive in" with few interruptions.
9. _____ I like to celebrate birthdays on a small scale, with only one or two close friends or family members.
10. _____ People describe me as "soft-spoken" or "mellow."
11. _____ I prefer not to show or discuss my work with others until it's finished.
12. _____ I dislike conflict.
13. _____ I do my best work on my own.
14. _____ I tend to think before I speak.
15. _____ I feel drained after being out and about, even if I've enjoyed myself.
16. _____ I often let calls go through to voice mail.
17. _____ If I had to choose, I'd prefer a weekend with absolutely nothing to do to one with too many things scheduled.
18. _____ I don't enjoy multitasking.
19. _____ I can concentrate easily.
20. _____ In classroom situations, I prefer lectures to seminars.

Scoring

Add up the number of "true" and "false" answers and place the totals in the spaces below.

NUMBER OF TRUE ANSWERS _____   NUMBER OF FALSE ANSWERS _____

The more often you answered "true," the more **introverted** you probably are. Given the choice, introverts will devote their social energy to a small group of people they care about most, preferring a glass of wine with a close friend to a party full of strangers. Introverts think before they speak, have a more deliberate approach to risk, and enjoy solitude. They feel energized when focusing deeply on a subject or activity that really interests them. When they're in overly stimulating environments (too loud, too crowded, and the like), they tend to feel overwhelmed. They seek out environments of peace, sanctuary, and beauty; they have an active inner life and are at their best when they tap into its riches.

The more often you answered "false," the more **extroverted** you probably are. Extroverts relish social life and are energized by interacting with friends and strangers alike. They're typically assertive, go-getting, and able to seize the day. Extroverts are great at thinking on their feet; they're relatively comfortable with conflict. Given the choice, extroverts usually prefer more stimulating environments that give them frequent opportunities to see and speak with others. When they're in quiet environments, they're prone to feeling bored and restless. They are actively engaged in the world around them and at their best when tapping into its energy.

If you found yourself with a roughly equal number of "true" and "false" answers, then you may be an **ambivert**, which means you fall in the middle of the introvert-extrovert spectrum. In many ways, ambiverts have the best of both worlds, able to tap into the strengths of both introverts and extroverts as needed.

"Until you make the unconscious conscious, it will direct your life and you will call it fate."

CARL JUNG,
SWISS PSYCHOANALYST

Based on the quiz, do you think you're an introvert, an extrovert, or an ambivert?

Were you surprised by the results of the quiz? In what way?

Ask a trusted friend or family member to give you their opinion of your personality style. What is their response? What factors might influence their opinion?

In what ways do you agree with your friend's interpretation and in what ways do your perspectives differ?

List some of the
important people
in your life—your
partner, friend,
colleague, or kids.
From your point of
view, where do they
fall on the introvert-
extrovert scale?

Even if you might think you are a true introvert or extrovert, that doesn't mean your behavior is predictable across all circumstances. This is partly because we are all gloriously complex individuals, but also because there are so many different kinds of introverts and extroverts.

List qualities, habits, and behaviors of yours that are representative of a classic introvert and those that are more typical of a true extrovert.

WAYS I'M AN INTROVERT

WAYS I'M AN EXTROVERT

People change
profoundly over time.
What are some of the
ways you've changed
in the past five years?

Maybe it's not so much that you're introverted in some ways and extroverted in others but that your behavior on this scale is situation-dependent. After all, behavior is a function of both personality and situation. Are you an introvert in some situations and an extrovert in others? Start noticing which situations bring out which qualities and keep track of them here.

SITUATIONS IN WHICH I BEHAVE LIKE AN INTROVERT

SITUATIONS IN WHICH I BEHAVE LIKE AN EXTROVERT

1.

2.

3.

What three factors might help you feel more confident in a situation that seems to go against your nature?

Rethinking Quiet

What childhood
memories do you
have of feeling as
if you were on the
sidelines? Did you
wish you could
join in or were
you comfortable
observing others?

"We tend to think showing vulnerability makes us seem weak, inadequate, and flawed—a mess. But when others see our vulnerability, they might perceive something quite different, something alluring."

EMILY ESFAHANI SMITH,
AUTHOR OF *THE POWER OF MEANING*

DATE   /   /

List some of the
words or phrases
you associate with
"introvert" and
"introversion."

Pick one word or phrase
from the list above that
you might think of as
negative. Rewrite it as
positive. How can this
quality lead to positive
outcomes?

22

Think of someone you know whom you might describe as shy or withdrawn. What is another way to describe this person that highlights their positive traits?

Even though we
can reach for the
outer limits of our
temperaments, it
can often be better
to situate ourselves
squarely inside our
comfort zones. Draw
your comfort zone,
whatever that might
mean to you.

Some animals carry their shelter wherever they go. Some humans are just the same.

If you like to do things in a slow and steady way, don't let others make you feel as if you have to race. If you enjoy depth, don't force yourself to seek breadth. If you prefer single tasking to multitasking, stick to your guns. Being relatively unmoved by rewards gives you the incalculable power to go your own way.

Do you enjoy depth? How so? In what ways can you carve out more time for single tasking?

Describe a time
in your life when
introverted behavior
proved to be an
advantage.

"Nowhere can a man find a retreat more peaceful or more free from trouble than his own soul."

MARCUS AURELIUS, *MEDITATIONS*

What kinds of retreats
do you seek?

One helpful way
to think about
introversion and
extroversion is in
terms of preferences
for certain levels
of stimulation.
Introverts tend to
prefer less external
stimulation, extroverts
more. With a better
understanding of your
optimum amount
of stimulation,
you can begin
consciously trying
to position yourself
in environments
favorable to your
personality—neither
overstimulating nor
understimulating,
neither boring nor
anxiety producing.

Describe a recent
situation in which you
felt overstimulated.
Where were you and
what were you doing?

Write about a recent
situation in which you
felt understimulated.
Where were you and
what were you doing?

What does being alone
feel like to you?

"Alone had always felt like an actual place to me, as if it weren't a state of being but rather a room where I could retreat to be who I really was."

CHERYL STRAYED, AUTHOR OF *WILD*

Describe a recent occasion when you felt confident. What were you doing?

Find out more about the creator of a work of art, music, or literature you love. Who is the creator and what works of theirs do you love? Do you think they would prefer solitude or more time with others?

Start paying attention
to the portrayal
of introverts in
movies you watch.
What kinds of
scenes show their
preference for quiet
and solitude? How is
their thoughtfulness
depicted as a gift?

From Ferdinand the
bull to Jane Eyre,
literature abounds
with introverts. Who
are some of your
favorites and why?

"Be a loner. That gives you time to wonder, to search for the truth. Have holy curiosity. Make your life worth living."

ALBERT EINSTEIN, THEORETICAL PHYSICIST

When and where is
quiet encouraged in
your life?

What are some
activities that
help you recharge
after a particularly
demanding day?
What are some of the
obstacles to engaging
in these activities,
and how might you
overcome them?

TIME	ACTIVITY	ENERGY LEVEL (1–10)
9:00 a.m.		
10:00 a.m.		
11:00 a.m.		
12:00 p.m.		
1:00 p.m.		
2:00 p.m.		
3:00 p.m.		
4:00 p.m.		
5:00 p.m.		
6:00 p.m.		
7:00 p.m.		
8:00 p.m.		

Finding Your Sweet Spots

For the next week, capture your hourly activities during the day on these pages, marking your energy level during each activity on a scale of 1 (low) to 10 (high). Pay close attention to the moments when you feel optimally stimulated. These are your Sweet Spots. At the end of every day, star every Sweet Spot that you can remember. Similarly, pay attention to the moments when you feel over- or understimulated. Put an x next to these moments.

DATE   /   /

TIME	ACTIVITY	ENERGY LEVEL (1–10)
9:00 a.m.		
10:00 a.m.		
11:00 a.m.		
12:00 p.m.		
1:00 p.m.		
2:00 p.m.		
3:00 p.m.		
4:00 p.m.		
5:00 p.m.		
6:00 p.m.		
7:00 p.m.		
8:00 p.m.		

TIME	ACTIVITY	ENERGY LEVEL (1–10)
9:00 a.m.		
10:00 a.m.		
11:00 a.m.		
12:00 p.m.		
1:00 p.m.		
2:00 p.m.		
3:00 p.m.		
4:00 p.m.		
5:00 p.m.		
6:00 p.m.		
7:00 p.m.		
8:00 p.m.		

DATE _____ / _____ / _____

TIME	ACTIVITY	ENERGY LEVEL (1–10)
9:00 a.m.		
10:00 a.m.		
11:00 a.m.		
12:00 p.m.		
1:00 p.m.		
2:00 p.m.		
3:00 p.m.		
4:00 p.m.		
5:00 p.m.		
6:00 p.m.		
7:00 p.m.		
8:00 p.m.		

TIME	ACTIVITY	ENERGY LEVEL (1–10)
9:00 a.m.		
10:00 a.m.		
11:00 a.m.		
12:00 p.m.		
1:00 p.m.		
2:00 p.m.		
3:00 p.m.		
4:00 p.m.		
5:00 p.m.		
6:00 p.m.		
7:00 p.m.		
8:00 p.m.		

DATE   /   /

TIME	ACTIVITY	ENERGY LEVEL (1–10)	
9:00 a.m.			
10:00 a.m.			
11:00 a.m.			
12:00 p.m.			
1:00 p.m.			
2:00 p.m.			
3:00 p.m.			
4:00 p.m.			
5:00 p.m.			
6:00 p.m.			
7:00 p.m.			
8:00 p.m.			

TIME	ACTIVITY	ENERGY LEVEL (1–10)
9:00 a.m.		
10:00 a.m.		
11:00 a.m.		
12:00 p.m.		
1:00 p.m.		
2:00 p.m.		
3:00 p.m.		
4:00 p.m.		
5:00 p.m.		
6:00 p.m.		
7:00 p.m.		
8:00 p.m.		

Now go back through your weekly tracker and note all the Sweet Spots you starred. Understanding and optimizing your Sweet Spots can increase your satisfaction in every area of your life. List them here.

Pinpointing the situations and activities in your day that bring about negative emotions can also give you insight into how you can reduce anxiety or frustration and increase your joy. Go back through your weekly tracker and note all the anxious moments you gave an *x*. List them here.

DATE   /   /

Reflecting on your
weekly tracker, do you
notice any patterns
about when you tend
to feel overstimulated?

Do you notice any
patterns for when
you tend to feel
understimulated?

What are three ways
you could maximize
the amount or length
of activities that boost
your energy?

1.

2.

3.

1.

2.

3.

What are three ways
you could minimize
the amount or length
of activities that drain
your energy?

DATE   /   /

What are some ideas
for setting up your
work, hobbies, and
social life so that you
spend as much time
inside your Sweet Spots
as possible?

YOUR WORK (OR SCHOOL):

YOUR HOBBIES:

YOUR SOCIAL LIFE:

What is one way you could build a Sweet Spot into your day tomorrow?

Space to Create

When do you set
aside time for quiet
reflection?

What are some strategies
for building more of these
protected moments into
your day?

Do you have any
rituals for tuning in
to your inner worlds?
What are they?

"The one thing that you have that nobody else has is you. Your voice, your mind, your story, your vision. So write and draw and build and play and dance and live as long as you can."

NEIL GAIMAN, AUTHOR AND FILMMAKER

If you could find a
free hour to devote
to a creative project
tonight, what would
it be?

Skip the committee meeting. Cross the street to avoid making aimless chitchat with random acquaintances. Read. Cook. Run. Write a story.

How can you make more space for yourself in the coming week, whether you devote it to the creative project you describe on the previous page or to something else that brings you joy?

When it comes to social activities that take time away from your personal projects, try to get an overall sense of how many you'd like to attend rather than making decisions on a case-by-case basis. This way, you don't feel guilty about declining those party invitations.

Pick a time frame that makes sense to you—week, month, or year—and make a plan for how many events you want to attend or host and how often you can stay home.

Look ahead at your calendar for the next month. List any social gatherings, including networking events, that you have coming up.

Which, if any, of these outings could be cut?

Give yourself
permission to politely
decline an invite
or request. Was the
outcome what you
had expected? Write
about the experience
here.

Describe the last
time you were able to
rejuvenate yourself.
Where were you and
what were you doing?

We know from myth that there are different strengths in the world. One child is given a light saber, another a wizard's education. The trick is not to amass all the different kinds of power, but to use well the kind you've been granted. List some of your unique strengths, taking care to include ones that might get overlooked by others.

Circle one strength you've listed that you'd like to build on. How can you devote at least a half hour this week to developing this talent further?

Who are your biggest
supporters? How do
they help lift you up?

"We do not believe in ourselves until someone reveals that deep inside us something is valuable, worth listening to, worthy of our trust, sacred to our touch."

E. E. CUMMINGS, AMERICAN POET

Describe a recent activity you were engaged in that required your intense attention. Did you enjoy it? Did you have enough time to pursue it fully?

Use your natural
powers—of persistence,
concentration, insight,
and sensitivity—to
do work you love and
work that matters.
What work do you
feel passionate about?

"Do not fear to be eccentric in opinion, for every opinion now accepted was once eccentric."

BERTRAND RUSSELL,
PHILOSOPHER AND SOCIAL CRITIC

What are your most
eccentric ideas or
opinions?

It can be tough for introverts to identify projects they're enthusiastic about. They have spent so much of their lives conforming to extroverted norms that by the time they choose a career or a calling, it feels normal to ignore their own preferences.

How did you find your career or calling? Was it something you chose, or was it chosen for you?

To hone your skill
at identifying your
passion, first start
paying attention to
your preferences. List
them here.

If you speak with conviction, it doesn't matter if you're quiet or loud, short or tall, masculine or feminine. So practice deciding what you think about things. Exercise this skill as you would any other muscle, even if you're simply arriving at an opinion of last night's movie. Write a short opinion piece here about a recent meal you had, book you read, or movie you saw.

What are two
strategies you could
employ for holding
on to your opinion
even when others
disagree with it?

DATE / /

What imperfections
of someone else can
you forgive today?

What imperfections of
your own can you forgive
today?

76

"One cannot arrive at true nobility of spirit if one is not prepared to forgive the imperfections of human nature."

HAZRAT INAYAT KHAN,
SUFI TEACHER AND MUSICIAN

"The most regretful people on earth are those who felt the call to creative work, who felt their own creative power restive and uprising, and gave to it neither power nor time."

MARY OLIVER, POET AND ESSAYIST

How do you feel
called to creative work
or a creative career?
How can you give
more energy and
time to this pursuit?

Identifying Your Core Personal Project

Unleashing a passion can transform a life. When you have work you care about deeply, you'll find you're able to act out of character in service of that work. The following pages will help you zero in on what acclaimed speaker Professor Brian Little calls your "core personal project."

What did you want to be when you grew up?

What about that choice appealed to you?

Describe the last time
you were able to act
out of character in
service of work you
cared about deeply.
What kind of work do
you gravitate toward?

Envy is an ugly
emotion, but it tells
the truth. Who do
you envy and what
do you desire?

What moves you to tears as it relates to your life's purpose?

Looking back over
your responses on
the previous pages,
brainstorm some areas
of overlap between
what you wanted to
be as a child, the work
you gravitate toward,
and the people and
positions you envy.

What core personal
project might exist
at the intersection
of these vectors?

Once you've identified
your calling, pursue
it with energy and
passion. Set a goal for
yourself: What would
you like to accomplish
and by when?

When you practice deliberately, a habit championed by Swedish psychologist Anders Ericsson, you identify the tasks or knowledge that are just out of your reach. You strive to upgrade your performance, monitor your progress, and revise accordingly. Practice sessions that fall short of this standard are not only less useful—they're counterproductive. They reinforce existing cognitive mechanisms instead of improving them.

What's one skill of yours that could benefit from more practice? When and where can you practice, and for how long? Write it into your schedule.

What are the benefits
of practicing alone?

What are the benefits of
practicing with someone
else?

"Our culture made a virtue of living only as extroverts. We discouraged the inner journey, the quest for a center. So we lost our center and have to find it again."

ANAÏS NIN, WRITER AND DIARIST

What tools could
help you on your
inner journey?

Put your busy,
imaginative brain
to work by picturing
your victory and
bolstering your
confidence. Draw a
picture that represents
your reaching a goal
as a result of your
practice.

How can you help someone else in your life recognize the power of their quiet?

In an ideal world, your work and life purpose would be one and the same, or at least connected in some way. For many people, however, it's not an ideal world. If that's the case for you, try to earn your income from work that doesn't take too much time and energy. Then you can spend the rest of the time doing what matters most.

What is your situation? How would you like to improve it?

If work is not connected to your life purpose, how can you spend more time doing what you love?

"Let us read, and let us dance; these two amusements will never do any harm to the world."

VOLTAIRE, WRITER, HISTORIAN, AND PHILOSOPHER

What other
amusements would
benefit you and the
world around you?

II.

USING
YOUR QUIET

How much time will it take to get to Carnegie Hall? I don't know. It doesn't matter. As with all such things, the fun is in the attempt.

∾

I HOPE YOU'VE NOW HAD A CHANCE to find out more about your personality type, and to explore some of your unique strengths. Ideally, you will have identified some projects you're passionate about and spent a little time working on them. If you're anything like me, you enjoy working alone and find energy and inspiration through solitude. However, most of us can't pursue our passions solely in a vacuum. We need to meet the world. Some of us have to speak for a living. In public. Some of us have to work in open-office plans and attend daily meetings. Almost all of us have colleagues, friends, and family members whose temperaments differ from ours.

Having found our quiet, our next focus is on learning how to use it and hold on to it despite the noise around us. Sometimes this will mean carving out space and creating boundaries so we can pursue our work in the style we find most comfortable. Other times, this will require increasing our confidence in areas that have historically made us nervous. In the following pages, you'll discover how to put your strengths to work for you in an extroverted world.

Leaving Your Comfort Zone

While in the first section of this journal you were invited to dive deep into your comfort zone, let's now think about your relationships with others, your workplace, your leadership potential, and your contribution to the world. To do that, you'll need to leave your comfort zone.

When (if ever) do you enjoy the spotlight—whether at work or home, with people you don't know or those with whom you're intimately acquainted?

When I talk with a stranger or a group of people, my smile is bright and my manner direct, but there's a split second that feels like I'm stepping onto a high wire.

Do you feel vulnerable when talking to or in front of others? What do you tell yourself in these situations?

What situations do you tend to avoid because you find them overstimulating? Considering both career and personal benefits, how might it benefit you (or not) to put yourself in overstimulating situations more often?

1.

2.

3.

4.

5.

List some instances where you feel pressured to appear more outgoing than you really are.

Which of the instances on the previous page are serving you and in which instances might you want to reconsider your behavior? For example, if you've learned to pretend you love giving presentations—and it's an important part of your job—perhaps that's a performance you want to keep. If, on the other hand, you are mingling more than you need to at office parties, perhaps that's a behavior you could reconsider.

What ideas or tasks
are you excited to
tackle this week?

"You may not control all the events that happen to you, but you can decide not to be reduced by them."

MAYA ANGELOU, POET, MEMOIRIST, AND CIVIL RIGHTS ACTIVIST

What is one part of
your typical day that
makes you anxious?
What could you do to
lessen your anxiety?

Describe one work
situation in which
being introverted
was an asset to you
and your team.
What qualities of
yours contributed
to the success of the
situation?

Today, try adding
your opinion to a
conversation where
you would normally
stay quiet. Write about
the experience here.

Ideas can be shared quietly; they can be communicated in writing; they can be packaged into highly produced lectures; they can be advanced by allies.

What is a new idea
you're eager to share,
whether at work, at
home, or in another
context? What is a way
you can share the idea
quietly to make sure
others hear what you
have to say?

Describe a recent situation in which you felt unable to get your point across to someone else. What were some of the factors preventing you from making your case?

What strategies might you employ next time to make your voice heard?

Writer and speaker Meagan Francis offers this advice for dealing with social anxiety: "If walking into a crowded room stresses you out, try getting there early. If possible, really early, when the tables are mostly empty and coordinators are still buzzing around the room, getting things ready." Try taking this advice the next time it applies, and write about your experience here.

How did this preparation ease your anxiety as compared to when you arrive on time or late?

"As luck would have it, assertiveness isn't a personality trait, like introversion or extroversion. Instead, assertiveness is something you do, not something you are. Assertiveness is learned, practiced, sometimes failed, and tried again, like riding a bike."

ELLEN HENDRIKSEN, CLINICAL PSYCHOLOGIST
AND AUTHOR OF *HOW TO BE YOURSELF*

Try being more assertive today in a situation in which you might typically have shied away. How did it go?

Observe another
introvert in conver-
sation and how they
asserted themselves
successfully. Describe
the reaction others
had and how you felt.

Write about an
upcoming occasion in
which you will need
to go outside your
comfort zone. What
are you feeling leading
up to this event?

What are some ways to
prepare yourself for this
occasion? How can you
draw on some of your
strengths to meet this
challenge?

Describe an instance
from your past when
talking less could
have helped your
cause.

"Those who know do not speak. Those who speak do not know."

LAO TZU,
ANCIENT CHINESE PHILOSOPHER

Navigating Relationships

Now that you've begun to work outside of your comfort zone in a way that's comfortable to you, let's consider one aspect of dealing with other people: relationships. In Finding Your Quiet, you began thinking about where some of the people close to you fall on the introvert-extrovert scale. If introverts and extroverts are at opposite ends of the spectrum, how can they possibly get along? Yet the two types are often drawn to each other—in friendship, business, and especially romance. These pairs can enjoy great excitement and mutual admiration, a sense that each completes the other. One tends to listen, the other to talk; one is sensitive to beauty, but also to slings and arrows, while the other barrels cheerfully through their days; one pays the bills and the other arranges the children's play dates. But it can also cause problems when members of these unions pull in opposite directions.

Next we're going to put some energy into thinking about how to build on the natural synergy of introvert-extrovert pairs and about how to handle some of the challenges arising from forces that pull in opposite directions. And not all relationships are ones you'll want to work on improving. Some you'll simply want to limit.

Love is essential; gregariousness is optional. Cherish your nearest and dearest. Work with colleagues you like and respect. Relationships make everyone happier, introverts included, but think quality over quantity.

What are some of the most successful examples of introvert-extrovert relationships that you've known? What strengths does each person bring to the relationship?

"I will protect my energy around draining people. I will learn how to set healthy boundaries."

JUDITH ORLOFF, PSYCHIATRIST AND
AUTHOR OF *THE EMPATH'S SURVIVAL GUIDE*

How can you protect
your energy today?
How will you set
healthy boundaries
with others?

Check in with yourself
at the end of the day.
Were you successful at
protecting your energy?
What boundaries could
you set for tomorrow?

What is one way
you manage an area
in which you're not
temperamentally
compatible with
someone close to you?

What is one area
that still needs
improvement in
how you manage
this incompatibility?

Describe someone
you know in your
work who appears to
be a natural introvert
who is effective at
their work. How do
they speak, stand, or
interact with others?

What qualities do
you have in common
with this person and
what skills are they
using that might come
naturally to you?

It can be hard
for extroverts to
understand how badly
introverts need to
recharge at the end
of a busy day. What
are three ideas for
gently letting a loved
one know you need a
little time to yourself?

1.

2.

3.

"Remember that when you take the time you need, you are happier, less stressed, and more engaged with your partner."

SARAH JONES, FOUNDER OF *INTROVERTED ALPHA*

Whether at the office
or at home, try
asking for time to
think when you feel
you need it before
giving someone an
immediate response.
How did you make
your request? What
was the result?

It's hard for introverts to understand just how hurtful their silence can be. Are there any instances in which your silence might be misinterpreted? Write about them here and brainstorm some solutions.

"Twice in two days, I have exercised the discipline to say nothing. Twice, the consequent silence has delivered an effective and creative solution to a seemingly overwhelming problem."

JEAN BABB, COACH AND STRATEGY CONSULTANT

Allow a pause in
conversation today
where you might
feel pressured to fill
in the silence. What
happens? How can
silence deliver a
solution?

Author of *The Small Talk Code* Gregory Peart claims, "When you act first to direct the conversation, you feel a sense of control. Shifting from a passive to an active mindset can truly change your world." Today, try acting first to initiate a conversation. How did it boost your confidence or give you a better sense of control?

Writer and editor Lindsay Hood recommends that you "gather a few tidbits to share ahead of time so you don't reply with the simple 'Oh, I'm fine' that leads to long, awkward silences. Two or three little snippets/anecdotes about yourself that happened in the last three to four months should do it."

Think of two or three anecdotes you can share with someone else in a social setting and write them here.

What are some topics you feel comfortable talking about? Write a few down and keep adding to the list as more occur to you.

"The comfort level I have with [a] topic will manifest itself as confidence."

GREGORY PEART, AUTHOR AND FOUNDER OF SOCIALUPGRADER.COM

Research suggests that
introverts like people
they meet in friendly
contexts; extroverts
tend to prefer those
they compete with.

LIST SOME PEOPLE YOU'VE MET IN FRIENDLY CONTEXTS:

LIST SOME PEOPLE YOU'VE MET IN COMPETITIVE CONTEXTS:

HOW HAVE THESE CONTEXTS INFLUENCED YOUR FIRST

IMPRESSIONS?

Anyone can be a great negotiator. It often pays to be quiet and gracious, to listen more than talk, and to have an instinct for harmony rather than conflict. Can you think of a situation in which listening and aiming for harmony have helped you reach a compromise with someone? Describe the conversation here.

Think of a tense dialogue you recently had with someone whose temperament conflicted with yours. What can you learn from the conflict?

What are some ways
you could support
someone in your life
who doesn't talk as
loud or fast as others?

Work

Often, one of the main places introverts are forced to adapt to an extrovert world is in their work. What I call the New Groupthink elevates teamwork above all else. It insists that creativity and intellectual achievement come from a gregarious place. This approach can take the form of open-plan offices or an emphasis on collaboration, which promotes interaction and often inhibits solitary work.

In what ways have you experienced the New Groupthink in your work?

What aspects of
your work fit your
personality style?

What aspects are not a
good fit?

Draw a diagram to
illustrate how your
school or workplace is
organized. Where are
the places that allow
for collaboration?
What about quiet
reflection? Keeping
your diagram in
mind, list three
ideas for optimizing
productivity within
the existing space.

Draw a diagram of
your ideal workspace,
including boundaries.

Can you implement
any changes or make
suggestions that would
help bring your workspace
closer to your ideal?

Writer Elan Morgan
notes that "pockets
of time and space can
be effectively carved
out to give you space
to breathe and, yes,
maybe even enjoy
your work again."

What "pockets of time and
space" can you carve out?

Describe the leadership style of your current boss or one you've had in the past. How quickly do they make decisions? How do they encourage group work and solo work? List three positive qualities you share with this person.

Restorative Niches

"Restorative Niche" is Professor Brian Little's term for the place you go after stretching outside your comfort zone when you want to return to your true self. It can be a physical place, like a path beside a river, or a temporal one, like the quiet breaks you plan between phone calls. It can mean canceling your social plans on the weekend before a big meeting at work, practicing yoga or meditation, or choosing e-mail over an in-person meeting.

What are some Restorative Niches you've already created for yourself? What more can you brainstorm?

TIME	ACTIVITY	
9:00 a.m.		
10:00 a.m.		
11:00 a.m.		
12:00 p.m.		
1:00 p.m.		
2:00 p.m.		
3:00 p.m.		
4:00 p.m.		
5:00 p.m.		
6:00 p.m.		
7:00 p.m.		
8:00 p.m.		

Look ahead to tomorrow's schedule. Write it out here. Schedule a few Restorative Niches and try to stick with your new schedule.

You can even create a Restorative Niche *during* a meeting with others by carefully selecting where you will sit and when and how you participate. Try this at your next meeting or social event. What happened? Would you do it again?

NAME	STRENGTHS	TASKS

We should actively seek out symbiotic introvert-extrovert relationships, in which leadership and other tasks are divided according to people's natural strengths and temperaments.

Think about some of the people on your team. What are their strengths and what tasks might fall most naturally to them? Who do you want to get to know a little better?

One
genuine
new
relationship
is worth
a fistful of
business
cards.

At a networking event, forget about working the room and aim instead for attempting to build one genuine new relationship. How did it go?

Leadership

Introverts ascend to leadership not because they're seeking to be leaders. They become leaders in service of their vision. Think of a successful leader who has a temperament similar to yours. Write a little about this person here. What qualities make them a strong leader?

How are you two similar? How are you different?

Would you like to take on more of a leadership role somewhere in your life?

If so, where? What challenges do you face stepping into this role?

How can quiet skills—like taking time to think, asking questions, empowering others, and thinking cooperatively—boost leadership?

Public Speaking

One of the most widely dreaded activities involved in many kinds of leadership opportunities is public speaking. It's also an area that will often further your core personal project (page 80), if only by helping you gain an audience and momentum for your cause.

The next time you have to speak publicly—even if only in front of a small group—think about how you can be yourself. How will you stay true to your nature?

Studies show that taking simple physical steps—like smiling—makes us feel stronger and happier, while frowning makes us feel worse. The next time you're in an intimidating situation, try smiling. Does it help? Write about your experience here.

Could learning to
overcome some of
your anxiety over
public speaking help
you in your career or
with your personal
goals? If so, how?

If you have a great sense of humor, use it. If you're not a natural cut-up, don't try to be. Instead, focus on what you do best. What are some of your strengths as a public speaker?

Try practicing a speech or presentation you need to give, or even the opening to a conversation if you happen to run into someone in the hall.

What are some ways you'd like to improve your delivery to be more effective?

What are some things you'd keep the same?

Watch an online video of a speech you admire, especially one given by a low-key but masterful presenter. What is their overall message? What story or example did they add to make the speech more relatable?

Think about what the speaker's audience wanted to hear. How did the speech give them what they wanted?

Thoughtful and
thought-provoking
are every bit as
powerful as dynamic
and entertaining.

What extra preparation
or rituals could help
you prepare to give a
presentation or a speech?

Try reframing an upcoming situation in which you need to give a public presentation. Instead of thinking about how you'll be judged and whether you'll be seen as "good enough," think about what you are bringing to your audience or what you are learning. What questions do you have about the subject material? What knowledge are you hoping to share?

We all have physical tics we revert to when uncomfortable—running our hands through our hair, adjusting our tie. Body language experts call these "unconscious adapters." Pay attention to the behaviors you revert to when you're uncomfortable. What are some of your unconscious adapters?

This week try minimizing these unconscious adapters, such as striving to eliminate "ums" and "ahs" from your verbal conversation. How were you able to note the behaviors and modify them? How did modifying them affect your experience of the conversation?

New research shows that verbal hesitation actually makes speakers more credible. Start paying attention to the pauses in other people's speaking. In your view, how does it affect their credibility? How does it affect your experience as the listener?

Some research suggests that expressing uncertainty makes people trust your opinions more. What do you think about voicing your uncertainty—do you find it useful, or do you feel it detracts from your message?

Your Contribution

We are driven out of our comfort zone by goals that cut to the core of our values and ideals. These, as you identified on page 80, are our "core personal projects." They surface when times call for it, such as when our families need extra care or when we are motivated to excel professionally.

Planning ahead for these core personal projects ensures you are able to fully tap into the power of your temperamental strengths and proactively address where you might need a little help to be your best self. Use the following prompts to prepare you for that next big stretch . . . and how to recuperate from it as well.

Why does this core
personal project
matter to you?

How will you leverage and
perhaps stretch beyond
your strengths for a
successful outcome? What
help will you need?

How can you put yourself in the lighting that's right for you?

The secret to life is to put yourself in the right lighting. For some it's a Broadway spotlight; for others, a lamp-lit desk.

If the gift you have to give the world requires public speaking or networking or other activities that make you uncomfortable, do them anyway. What activities associated with your core personal project are comfortable for you? Which ones are uncomfortable?

Accept that some
necessary activities
will be difficult, get
the training you need
to make them easier,
and reward yourself
when you're done.
What training do you
need to accomplish
your core personal
projects and what
is your first step to
gaining access to it?

Figure out what you are meant to contribute to the world and make sure you contribute it.

What are you meant
to contribute to the
world? What is one
activity you could do
this week to further
that contribution?

What do the benchmarks for success look like for you, and what rewards will you give yourself for meeting them along the way?

Look back to your
Sweet Spots from
pages 41–47. How
have you been able to
implement more of
them into your day?
What other steps can
you take to increase
your joy this week?

Isn't it strange how deeply we mistrust quiet these days even though silence and solitude are widely held values in most spiritual traditions?

How will you help to promote silence and solitude—either at home or at work?

"I have to remind myself that my talents lie in deep analysis, reflective thinking, and quality over quantity—not in running around doing all the things."

JENNIFER GRANNEMAN, AUTHOR OF *THE SECRET LIVES OF INTROVERTS*

If there's one thing introverts love to do, it's learn. They also love to feel valuable and to share their knowledge with others. What is one thing you would like to learn more about?

How can you better
share your knowledge
with others?

"You have power over your mind— not outside events. Realize this, and you will find strength."

MARCUS AURELIUS, *MEDITATIONS*

DATE   /   /

What are some things you can take off your plate? How might you go about giving up these tasks?

183

DATE / /

As Cambridge University professor and Quiet Revolution advisory board member Dr. Brian Little explains, we are born with certain personality traits (our "fixed traits") and then develop others (our "free traits"). The introverted father at the party and the extroverted doctoral student in the library are both "exercising free traits"—the noble choice to act out of character and rise to the occasion. How will you exercise your free traits this week?

TIME	ACTIVITY
9:00 a.m.	
10:00 a.m.	
11:00 a.m.	
12:00 p.m.	
1:00 p.m.	
2:00 p.m.	
3:00 p.m.	
4:00 p.m.	
5:00 p.m.	
6:00 p.m.	
7:00 p.m.	
8:00 p.m.	

Use the schedules on the following pages to plan your week, identifying Sweet Spots, scheduling Restorative Niches, and limiting the number of outings you commit to.

TIME	ACTIVITY
9:00 a.m.	
10:00 a.m.	
11:00 a.m.	
12:00 p.m.	
1:00 p.m.	
2:00 p.m.	
3:00 p.m.	
4:00 p.m.	
5:00 p.m.	
6:00 p.m.	
7:00 p.m.	
8:00 p.m.	

TIME	ACTIVITY
9:00 a.m.	
10:00 a.m.	
11:00 a.m.	
12:00 p.m.	
1:00 p.m.	
2:00 p.m.	
3:00 p.m.	
4:00 p.m.	
5:00 p.m.	
6:00 p.m.	
7:00 p.m.	
8:00 p.m.	

DATE   /   /

TIME	ACTIVITY
9:00 a.m.	
10:00 a.m.	
11:00 a.m.	
12:00 p.m.	
1:00 p.m.	
2:00 p.m.	
3:00 p.m.	
4:00 p.m.	
5:00 p.m.	
6:00 p.m.	
7:00 p.m.	
8:00 p.m.	

TIME	ACTIVITY
9:00 a.m.	
10:00 a.m.	
11:00 a.m.	
12:00 p.m.	
1:00 p.m.	
2:00 p.m.	
3:00 p.m.	
4:00 p.m.	
5:00 p.m.	
6:00 p.m.	
7:00 p.m.	
8:00 p.m.	

DATE _____ / _____ / _____

TIME	ACTIVITY
9:00 a.m.	
10:00 a.m.	
11:00 a.m.	
12:00 p.m.	
1:00 p.m.	
2:00 p.m.	
3:00 p.m.	
4:00 p.m.	
5:00 p.m.	
6:00 p.m.	
7:00 p.m.	
8:00 p.m.	

TIME	ACTIVITY
9:00 a.m.	
10:00 a.m.	
11:00 a.m.	
12:00 p.m.	
1:00 p.m.	
2:00 p.m.	
3:00 p.m.	
4:00 p.m.	
5:00 p.m.	
6:00 p.m.	
7:00 p.m.	
8:00 p.m.	

PENGUIN LIFE

UK I USA I Canada I Ireland I Australia
India I New Zealand I South Africa

Penguin Life is part of the Penguin Random House group of companies
whose addresses can be found at global.penguinrandomhouse.com.

First published in the United States of America by Clarkson Potter/Publishers,
an imprint of Random House, a division of Penguin Random House LLC, New York 2019
First published in Great Britain by Penguin Life 2020
001

Copyright © Susan Cain, 2012, 2019

The moral right of the author has been asserted

Printed and bound in Great Britain by Clays Ltd, Elcograf S.p.A.

A CIP catalogue record for this book is available from the British Library

ISBN: 978–0–241–43924–1

www.greenpenguin.co.uk